UNTIMELY DEMISES

49½ poems with sticky endings

Written and illustrated
by Tim Cordell

Disclaimer

Any resemblance between the characters in this book and persons ~~living or~~ dead is highly unlikely, and damned unfortunate if so.

Visitations or contact may be made through the following mediums:

cordellcartoons.com

untimelydemises@gmail.com

Copyright © Tim Cordell

Jock's Sock

Jock thought black holes
were a load of old crock
till he was sucked into one
that had formed in the toe of his sock

Hamish

Hamish fell in love with a goldfish
though it was a short-lived affair
She could only live in water
he could only breathe in air

Now their different states of matter
didn't matter to his mind
nor the natter of the neighbours
carping 'Stick to your own kind!'

But Hamish should have known he was asking for trouble
when he blew her a kiss and she blew back a bubble

Love-bitten, fish-smitten,
helpless as a drowning kitten,
Hamish lost all self-control
and dived headfirst into her goldfish bowl

His head stuck fast and sealed him in
but he wouldn't smash the glass to save his own skin

For Hamish was no bounder in matters of the heart
and feared his love would flounder if he broke her bowl apart

So he breathed in water and blew out air
as the fish hid her tears in the reeds of his hair

And when Hamish blub-bubbled his final exhale
she waved him goodbye with a swish of her tail

Rhonda's Belt

Rhonda wore an anaconda for a belt
It made her curvaceous, it made her svelte

Tight round the middle, it continued to squeeze
till out popped Rhonda's brain,
with a sound like a sneeze

Professor Malone

The greatest inventor the world has never known
was the briefly celebrated Professor Malone
He invented a working time machine
that ran on farts and gasoline

But his very first journey was one he'd relive to regret
as he attempted to stop himself smoking his first cigarette

He arrived in his old bedroom, quite uninvited,
to witness the flick of a bic, as his cig was ignited

Sadly, the one thing the professor hadn't foreseen
was the grave consequence of not going green

His machine's noxious gases filled the room
and with one drag on the fag, his whole world went ka-boom!

His body was left fried and twisted,
though in another dimension, he never died nor existed

Escher Jnr.

When Escher Jnr. misbehaved
he was sent up to bed
and an early grave

Boris

Boris the ignoble parliamentarian,
made a pass at a mobile librarian

The dirty backbencher then tried to French her,
but his tongue got caught in an ill-fitting denture

He swallowed her teeth and came to grief
Verdict: Death by Missed Adventure

Phil's Filthy Sleeping Bag

Somewhere in Somerset, in a field near Stonehenge
Phil's filthy sleeping bag wakes up in a tent, intent on revenge

Coiled like the doings in a festival loo
and soiled by all manner of indigestible food
it sits in a lagoon of bodily fluids
communing with the moon and the ancient Druids

And hey presto! Just like that
the bag shape-shifts into an intestinal tract;
a tubular vessel made of flesh but no bones
with a mouth as flappy as Sylvester Stallone's

From that slobbering gob, acidic juices drip
as fingers fumble to undo the tent's outer zip

Then in trips Phil, ripped to the gills
reeking of booze and rattling with pills

In the dark, he lies on his back, kicks off his shoes
and sticks his feet into that big sac of ooze

The slippery lips open wide
and like a birth-in-reverse suck Phil inside,
where a gastric acid trip leaves him liquefied

But before turning back into a sleeping bag,
the intestinal tract has one last gag
as it convulses and coughs up Phil's security tag

Specky Jim

Specky Jim, just on a whim,
invited a dolphin for a swim

The daffy dolphin, just for a lark,
switched places with a Great White shark

Heather's Feathers

Joan and Heather got into a pillow fight
over whether foam or feather fillings
led to a sleep-filled night

Joan plumped for foam, with its scientific credentials
and the way it would shape itself round her bare essentials

Heather's fancy, however, was more tickled by feathers

"Polyurethane in a counterpane? Oh, goodness me, never!"

"You sound like a snooty cow from down south!"
cried Joan, spitting feathers, and foaming at the mouth

"How dare you speak so out of place!" shot back Heather,
slapping a cotton-slipped pillow into Joan's angry face

"Didn't feel a thing, you featherweight!"
said Joan, taking a swing that could – and did – decapitate

Not being a wound easily cauterised,
Joan was left feeling queasy and quite traumatised

But just to be sure, lest she should ever forget,
impressed on her pillow was a silhouette

Set in foam forever, with an admonishing frown
was the face of Heather, the girl who loved feathers
but didn't duck down

Bernie the Attorney

Bernie the attorney
had set off on a journey
when a dubious case blew up in his face
and he ended up on a gurney

Vinnie the Vintner

Vinnie the Vintner made wine in winter,
treading sour grapes
In over his head, he slipped into the red
and things corkscrewed out of shape

Nobody would drink his fermented resentment
or sink his bottled woes
They said "Your wine doesn't lead to contentment,
or appeal to the nose"

Unable to cope with being the butt of the joke
whom all the critics hated
Vinnie sealed himself in a vat made of oak
until his business was liquidated

When people enquired how Vinnie expired
they were told Vinnie vanished without trace
And all he'd left behind was a barrel of wine
with a rather bitter aftertaste

Milly

Milly was a social-media multi-tasker
who posted a posthumous upload
of herself getting multi-plastered,
all across the road

Mr Boon

Mr Boon was a complete buffoon,
who liked to eat blown-up balloons
He'd bite deep into their rubbery skin
and feel them burst inside of him
It made him happy, it made him grin,
it pumped him full of adrenaline

Then one day a chum gave Mr Boon a balloon,
stretched tight as a drum and as bright as the moon
He said "I know a dude who can deal you some,
if you really dig this heli-um…"

The silvery orbs slipped down a treat,
"Helium gets me high!" Mr Boon squeaked
Soon those balloons were all he would eat
and in no time at all, they changed his physique

His pants grew tight, his girth grew wide,
he started expanding on every side
But as Mr Boon ballooned in size,
he felt himself begin to rise

"Well, blow me! I feel lighter than air!"
he cried in alarm, floating up from his chair
Unmoored from the floor, he rose to the ceiling,
where his bloated body started bouncing and reeling

"You've overdosed on my gas-filled balloons!"
said the helium dealer, grabbing his harpoon
"There's only one way to make this thing stop"

And Mr Boon's life was rounded with a jab and a 'pop'

This is what happens to helium dealer squealers!

Unsteady Eddie

Unsteady Eddie picked up a sports whistle,
ready and set to blow

But he got mixed up with a starting pistol,
and Eddie's head, it go

Steve

Steve was caught up in a break-in
whilst at the butcher's shop
when some swines stole all the bacon
and purloined all the chops

The greedy thieves then hog-tied Steve
with a string of chipolatas
and told him "If you squeal to the pigs,
we'll have your guts for garters!"

Not possessing a stomach for evisceration
Steve attempted to ease the sausage-hostage situation

"Come on guys, please play nicer
...or I'll get mean and tough"

But they fed him through the bacon slicer,
and he tasted lean enough

Donny the Zombie

Donny was a zombie,
and a cheerful one at that
Always wore a toothy grin
and a funny little hat

But people didn't like him,
they said 'We'd rather see you dead!'
So Donny, being ever obliging,
pulled off his very own head

Cath

Cath's sole ambition
as a mathematician
was to eat the whole of pi

Yet everytime she took a bite
the numbers would multiply

It's said she choked
on the square root of x,
but no one could work out y

Harold's Particularity

Harold was particular
about all things perpendicular

So when an arrow struck him straight between the eyes
"Bravo! Good shot!" was all that he cried

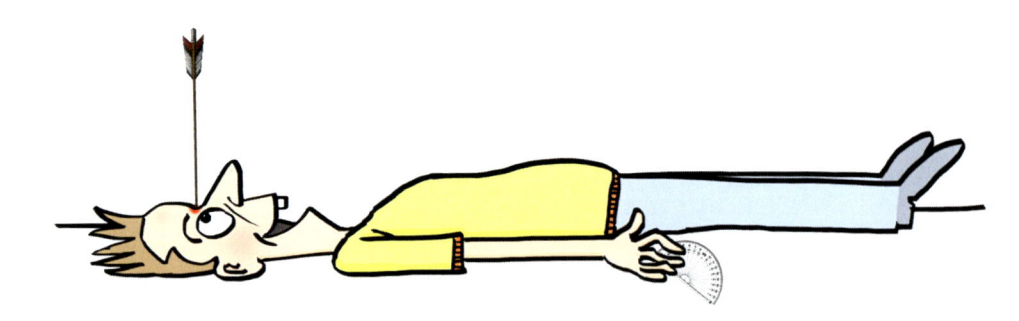

Granny Annie

Annie the green-fingered granny
could make a garden grow
Her skills herbaceous bordered on audacious
and her climbers would give you vertigo

But the weeds, feeling persecuted,
got together and concurred,
they'd had enough of being uprooted
and cut back by secateurs

So as Annie tamed the dandelions
and raked up all the leaves,
those weeds, with a grip of iron,
snaked up her legs and sleeves

In green shoots and roots Annie was bound,
in a cocoon from which no one could prise her
Leaving only her boots, she was pulled underground
and turned into fertilizer

Keith

Dressed in beige and picking sage,
whilst passing judgement in silent rage,
Keith keeled over in the garden centre
and died of middle age

Johnny's Big Beard

Johnny had a great big beard
that looked just like a nest
Birds would come and sit in there
and have a little rest

One day in moved a cuckoo
who stared Johnny in the eye

"This beard ain't big enough for two,"
he said, "you're going to have to fly"

"And just how," asked Johnny, "do you propose
to take this beard from under my nose?"

"You'll see," said the cuckoo before he disappeared,
burrowing deep into Johnny's big beard

Now every time Johnny tried to eat,
out popped the cuckoo with a wide-open beak

He snapped at every scrap, morsel and bite,
till Johnny was too weak to put up a fight

Sure enough, the cuckoo soon had his new home,
that he shared with no one, except Johnny's old bones

Reggie's Wedgie

Reggie got a wedgie
off a flexi-necked giraffe,
but the ferocity of the velocity
ripped poor Reggie in half

Herr Hess

Herr Hess was an evil dictator
who loved to process live data
The way that it flowed
to a well-ordered code
made him feel like a great liberator

But the data was raw
and felt brutalised
it despised being stored
and digitised
it was a hater of all that Herr Hess analysed
that mad creator of the homogenised

So whilst still coarse and unrefined
a rogue code breached the firewall of Hess's mind
It filled his brain like a barn fills a shed
and made Hess kill himself with a reboot to the head

Rocky

Rocky loved shadow boxing
You could say he was quite attached
But when he fought the shadow of his former self
he finally met his match

That blurry-lined smudge
held a well-defined grudge
at having never been a contender
And in a flurry of blows, it laid Rocky low
and looking like he'd been through a blender

You lightweight

Faith

Faith the fortune-teller had a run of bad luck
On the day she caught salmonella
she was hit by a ten-ton truck

She never saw it coming
or so they say
Well, I guess even a fortune-teller
can have a less than medium day

Clifford the ex-Wizard

Clifford was thrown out of wizard school
for failing to cast a spell
So he tried his luck as a conductor,
hoping nobody could tell

He ditched his wand and picked up the baton
(but for dramatic effect, kept his pointy hat on)
Then he stood at the podium, dressed all in black
and waved his arms like a maniac

But the musicians weren't happy with the maestro of deception
misconducting them all with his misdirection
Tempos were lost, sharp notes exchanged,
there were scores to be settled and rearranged

So all together on the count of 3,
the players all played the note of G

Oh, when that Major G force hit,
Clifford quivered and quavered a bit,
before toppling from his podium and into the pit

In that den of din, they did him in,
because for musos the fake shake of a stick was a sin

They sat on his baton and squashed his hat
and took turns on the cello to hammer him flat

Cue the final curtain, everyone cheers
that swizzling wizard had disappeared

Charlie Potts

At the age of 64,
Charlie Potts took up parkour

He said "I want to be known as 'Charlie the Cat'"

But everyone remembers him as 'that bloke who went splat'

Bridget the Fidget

Bridget the Fidget was a sculptor's model
who couldn't hold a pose
She'd twiddle her digits and start to wobble
and try to scratch her nose

(and just as an added distraction, she sometimes
did it with her toes)

Bit by bit, Bridget chip-chip-chipped
at the sculptor's cool veneer
till one twitch of her lip and he finally flipped
and Bridget froze in fear

Worried she'd recover
and there'd be merry hell to pay
the sculptor hurriedly smothered her
in the fastest-setting clay

And as soon as Bridget was hardened
he had her baked and glazed
Now she stands out in his garden,
looking beautiful and braised

Funny Frankie

Frankie was a funny guy
the joker of his group
And funnily enough, he choked on a fly
that was swimming in his soup

Frederique

Frederique loved to play hide-and-seek
He hid in a fridge and wasn't found for a week

When they opened the door, his body slid to the floor
and his mum broke the ice with a shriek

As the claws of Frederique's fingers began to thaw,
they opened to reveal a note that was hard to ignore

In shaky writing you could barely discern
his rigid digits had scrawled... 'Your turn!'

Jayne

Wayne was insane about Jayne
though she thought he was a bit of a creep
He said "This is how it feels to fall head-over-heels"
and he pushed her off Lover's Leap

Felicity

Felicity ate food off the floor
didn't care what had been there before;
dogs' bums, cats' paws,
dirty old boots from the Great Outdoors

She said the trick was to stick to the 5-second-rule
to make the chance of getting sick really miniscule

So when a dropped Weetabix stayed down for six
Felicity found herself in a bit of a fix

Throwing caution to the wind, she decided to risk it
and took a little nibble of that old wheaty biscuit

If only she'd left it for one second less
her story wouldn't be such a chiller

But no, she chose to ingest a mouthful of pests
and fell victim to the cereal killer

Lynne the Torch Singer

Lynne was a torch singer
and a parochial star
whose croaky, smoky vocals
entertained the yokels
in her local karaoke bar

But one night the diva with the grief-stricken groan
grabbed hold of a faulty microphone
'Torch Singer on Fire!' was the headline splash
after Lynne was electrocuted
and reconstituted
as a smouldering pile of ash

Mary Lou

Mary Lou took a trip to the zoo,
wearing her hair in a bun

In the elephants' enclosure,
they lost their composure
and the end was a sticky one

Colin's Magic Coin

Colin found a magic coin
lying in the dirt
He picked it up and rubbed it clean
with the corner of his shirt

To Colin's surprise,
right before his eyes,
a genie did appear

"You've got 3 wishes, mate," he said
"You better choose them all with care"

"Well, knock me down with a feather!
cried Colin,"Stone me! I'll be damned!"

"Bad choice," said the genie to Colin,
granting all 3 wishes with a wave of his hand

Wendy the Worrywart

Wendy was a worrywart
who took up yoga to calm her thoughts

A diet of Dyhana and several Asanas
made Wendy as bendy as a bunch of bananas

To avoid getting caught up in her wretched whims
she'd contort her body and stretch her limbs

And when Wendy tied herself into an impossible knot
she just breathed very deeply and waited to rot

Thelonious

Thelonious was in a one-man band
that never had a hit
And when things turned acrimonious
it caused the band to split

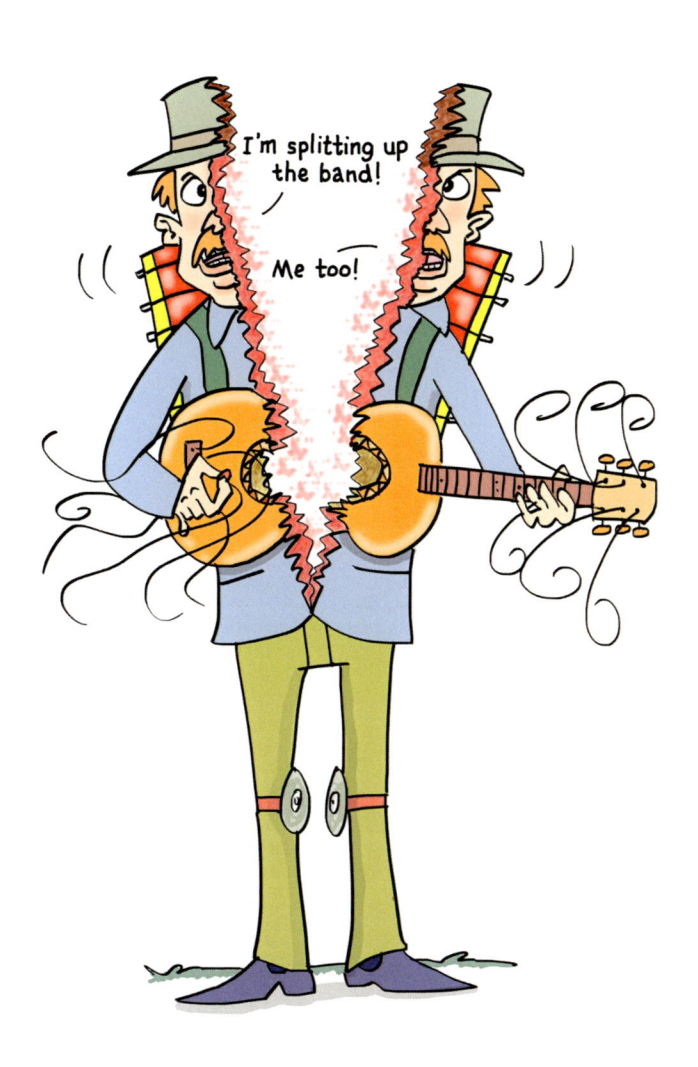

Max

Max had a thing about cats
and the thing that he had was a liking
for licking their backs

From the scruff of their necks to the tuft of their tails,
his tongue slipped along that old fur trail

Whether scabby-spined tabbies, covered in burrs
or well-refined felines, sweet as liqueur

there was no back his tongue wouldn't endure
so long as those cats continued to purr

But it was in the depths of a Himalayan
Max was discovered, tongue still flaying

Lost to all reason and out of his head
unaware it was the season a Himalayan shed

As his face turned a shade of Persian blue
Max knew he'd licked off far more than he could chew

And so he choked and croaked, hairball in his throat,
facedown in that purebred's basket

He was buried in Tibet, along with his pet,
in a plush coat and a fur-lined casket

An Astronaut

An astronaut had second thoughts
on a one-way trip to Mars
So he cried "Abort!" and abandoned ship
and stepped out among the stars

Lester the Protestor

Lester was an old-school protestor
who carried a placard and wore polyester
The voice of dissent wherever he went
with the heart of a corporate investor

On every topic, he grew misanthropic
if it got him started, he'd march to stop it

He was anti-monkeys climbing trees
anti-fish swimming in seas
About as anti-establishment as anti-freeze
with no anti-dote to his own dis-ease

He went anti-deodorant just to cause a stink
He was anti-quated in the ways that he'd think
He was the anti-christ of anti-love
He was anti-antipasti and all that stuff

The antithesis of anti-prejudice
he spouted bile from every orifice
No anti-sceptic heretic,
his was a highly toxic rhetoric

Oh yeah, Lester upped the ante
when it came to man's depravity
possessed with all the levity of a cavity
on a bloated corpse's face

But that blaggard with his placard
still made the world a better place,
when he turned anti-gravity
and floated into space

Dim-witted Dean

Dim-witted Dean was a green activist
whose sense of reality was somewhat amiss
He invented a way of drying your hands
that he claimed would cause less harm to the land

"We'll use hot air from an angry bull's nose,
and the more we annoy him, the hotter it blows!"

Needless to say, Dean was gored to death,
muttering "If only I'd gone with the Labrador's breath"

Gross Rose

Gross Rose ate snot from her nose,
wax from her ears
and jam from her toes

She stuffed her face with fluff from her belly,
chewed tags of loose flesh that wobbled like jelly
She feasted on flakes from crusty boils,
crunched gritty short snakes made of fingernail soil

Crumbs found in crannies,
hairs caught in cracks,
Yes, these were a few of her favourite snacks

She tucked into dirt nuggets, rolled under her chin,
dined on dead bugs from the folds of her skin

But none of these things were half as bad
as what the coroner discovered in the fatal kebab

Grandpa Pat

Grandpa Pat was an acrobat
with a pair of dodgy knees
So, fair to say, it didn't take all that
to dislodge him from his trapeze

(and just for the record, it only took a sneeze)

But as Pat fell, bones snapping
no one could tell, so they kept on clapping

Broken and disjointed,
he crashed onto the mat
leaving the crowd disappointed
things had ended so flat

Jack's Bucket List

Jack had a bucket list he was dying to fulfill,
so he asked Jill if she was up for it
on top of Blueberry Hill

"Last time I went up that hill
I was with Fats Domino,
and frankly, Jack, compared to you,
he was a real Romeo"

"Jill, you know I'm not the sort of bloke
who'd ever kiss and tell
So how about a drink with me,
I know a lovely little well?"

Jill agreed, on one condition;
there'd be no funny stuff,
without permission

Jack was quick to acquiesce,
but tried it on, nonetheless

"I warned you Jack, now you're going down!"
And with a swing of her pail, Jill broke his crown

Ding-dong bell went Jack's skull,
as his legs went floppy and his mind went dull

He felt himself falling, but not for Jill,
and the smack of the water provided no thrill

It was the end of the game, and he'd been outmatched
Well and truly shafted, no strings attached

Kelly's Calling

Kelly had a calling for bingo
Never had a win, though she knew all the lingo

She'd sit at the back of draughty halls
clucking for the clack of the tumbling balls

Eyes down, heart full of hope
the bingo caller coughs and clears his throat

Two little ducks! Everyone quack!

Two fat ladies! Too many snacks!

Legs eleven! Better not whistle,
 or they'll call HR for an instant dismissal

Snakes alive! It's 55!
Kelly has a heart attack! She's barely alive!

Talk about bad luck, Kelly's was worse,
her numbers came up and the caller cried "Hearse!"

Celeste's Heavenly Body

The heavenly body with which Celeste was blessed
made intellects wrecks and drove priests to confess
Even starry-eyed astronomers were known to profess
that cosmic phenomena didn't quite so impress

But nobody's knickers were more in a twist
than Artie the Particle Physicist

Subject to forces he couldn't resist
in parts of his body he thought didn't exist
Artie puckered his lips and moved in for the kiss

But his scientific experiment in human affection
only ended in tears and utter dejection
causing Artie to pause for a lifetime's reflection
before strapping Celeste to a slab
for a closer inspection

In a spirit decidedly misanthropic
Artie took a scalpel to his favourite poppet
And with a final cry of "Oh Artie, please stop it!"
Celeste was sliced very thinly
and made microscopic

Oh Celeste,
I love you to bits

Nora the Nun

Nora the nun took a vow of silence,
but the noises she made
drove the Sisters to violence

She'd slurp as she supped,
eat, burp and erupt,
smacking her lips
as the grub bubbled up

She'd cluck her tongue,
gasp for air,
and the rasp of her lungs
brought the nuns to despair

Though the straw that broke the camel's back
and forced the Sisters to attack
was the click of Nora's knuckle-crack

The Sisters showed Nora no mercy
pressing a prayer pillow to her face
and they only let go when certain
she'd passed on to a better place

But Nora left a final epistle
as she shuffled off this coil;
one last, long gassy whistle,
like a kettle on the boil

Bea

Bea was hard up for honey
Barely had enough to spread a round
And what was left had gone all runny
and turned a yellower shade of brown

Unable to survive so honey-deprived
Bea did what had to be done
and set off to sting a beehive
with a stocking and a smoking gun

But as royally-appointed nectar protectors,
the bizzies had installed smoke detectors
So Bea's sticky-up job came unstuck
though that wasn't the end of her run of bad luck

Her robber's stocking was so poorly made
it had more ladders than the fire brigade

At every rung, a honeybee stung
till Bea's face grew bigger than her bum

She tried to cry 'Help!' but the bees had her tongue
and her words came out as more of a hum

Hmm...it seemed Bea had paid a very high price
for her bumbling, bungled beehive heist

Stung to high heaven, to save a few quid
but no longer dying for honey, because she already did

Bobbing Bobby

Bobby was bobbing for apples
in the font of his local chapel

"Dear Mother of God, you cheeky young sod!"
cried the priest, as they started to grapple

"Why, I'll teach you some etiquette"
he said, grabbing Bobby by the scruff of the neck
"That's quite enough of your disrespect,
it's time for a baptism you'll never forget"

And with a bit of 'Our Father' and a quick 'Amen'
he held Bobby's head under, till he was unborn again

The Poet

When the poet called upon his muse
she duly appeared, only to give him abuse

"You're a knock-off Roger McGough" she scoffed,
"with a stump-blunt wit and ears made of cloth

You're as da-DUM, da-DUM, da-DUM as a post,
so put down your pen and give up the ghost"

But the poet, not being one for compliance,
chose to write on, in an act of defiance

"This barking mad doggerel has got to stop!"
cried the muse, striking the poet with a Writer's Block

The deadly blow was delivered without repentance,
killing the poet mid-flow and his poem mid-

The Sticky End

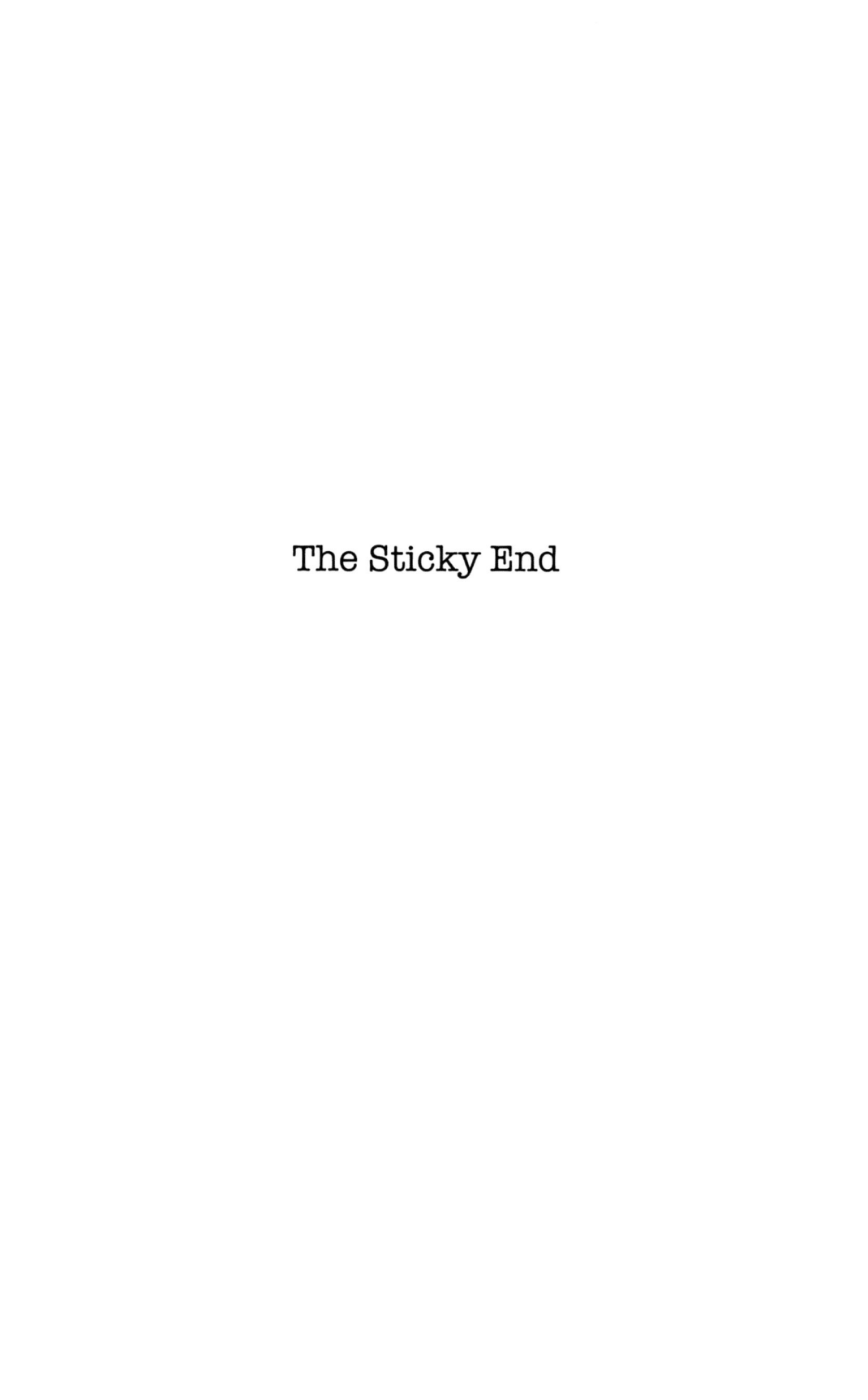